INTRODUCTION:

Our world is filled with complexities and conflicts, the art of mediation stands as a beacon of light, offering a path towards resolution, understanding, and harmony. Welcome to "The Art of Mediating Gracefully," a guide that will delve into the transformative power of mediation in both our personal and business lives.

Mediation is not merely a tool for conflict resolution; it is a profound practice that embodies the principles of empathy, communication, and collaboration. At its core, mediation is about facilitating dialogue between conflicting parties in a neutral and impartial manner, with the goal of reaching a mutually acceptable solution.

The art of mediation goes beyond simply resolving disputes; it cultivates a culture of respect, empathy, and understanding. By encouraging open communication and active listening, mediation can bridge divides, mend relationships, and pave the way for peaceful coexistence.

In our personal lives, conflicts are inevitable. Whether it's a disagreement with a loved one, a misunderstanding with a friend, or a rift within a family, conflicts can take a toll on our emotional well-being and relationships. This is where mediation plays a crucial role.

By embracing the principles of mediation, we can transform conflicts into opportunities for growth and understanding. Through effective communication, empathy, and negotiation, we can navigate challenging situations with grace and compassion, fostering stronger connections and deeper relationships.

In the fast-paced world of business, conflicts can arise from differing interests, goals, and perspectives. These conflicts, if left unresolved, can hinder productivity, damage morale, and impede progress. This is where mediation becomes indispensable.

In the business world, mediation offers a cost-effective and efficient alternative to lengthy and costly legal battles. By engaging in mediation, businesses can address conflicts swiftly, preserve relationships, and focus on their core objectives. Moreover, mediation can foster a culture of collaboration and teamwork, enhancing creativity, innovation, and organizational success.

As we embark on this journey into the art of mediating gracefully, let us remember that mediation is not just a tool; it is a mindset, a way of being in the world. By embracing the principles of mediation in our personal and business lives, we can cultivate understanding, harmony, and grace in all our interactions.

Join me as we explore the transformative power of mediation and discover how it can enrich our lives, deepen our relationships, and pave the way for a more peaceful and harmonious world.

DEDICATION:

It is important to understand that conflict arises every single day in our lives. We deal with it every day, even if we don't know it. I dedicate this book to every mom and dad that begin their day in meditation with their children. Every minister that deals with conflicts with their flock. Every business individual who deals with conflict inside and outside the office. You are brave individuals and I hope this book finds a place in your mediation heart. Go out and meditate.

The Power of Grace in Mediation

In the world of conflict resolution, mediation stands out as a powerful tool for fostering understanding, communication, and ultimately, peace. At the heart of successful mediation lies the concept of grace—a quality that encompasses generosity, respect, action, compassion, and energy. When these attributes are present in a mediation process, they can transform discord into harmony and hostility into cooperation.

G is for Generosity

Generosity is the cornerstone of grace in mediation. It is the willingness to go above and beyond for others, to listen with an open heart, and to offer understanding and empathy without judgment. In the midst of conflict, generosity can break down barriers and create space for mutual respect and understanding to flourish. A mediator who embodies generosity sets the tone for a constructive dialogue where all parties feel heard and valued.

R is for Respect

Respect is the bedrock of any successful mediation process. It involves recognizing the inherent dignity of every individual involved in the conflict, regardless of their background or perspective. When respect is present, communication becomes more meaningful, and solutions can be reached with integrity and fairness. A mediator who upholds respect creates a safe and inclusive environment where all voices are heard and valued.

A is for Action

Action is the mechanism for change in mediation. It involves identifying common goals, exploring creative solutions, and guiding parties towards mutually beneficial agreements. A mediator who takes decisive action can help parties move past impasse and find a path forward towards resolution. By encouraging proactive steps and fostering a sense of progress, the mediator empowers parties to take ownership of the mediation process and shape their own future.

C is for Compassion

Compassion is the heartbeat of grace in mediation. It is the deep-seated concern for the well-being of others and the recognition of shared humanity in the face of conflict. A compassionate mediator listens not only to words but also to emotions, seeking to understand the underlying needs and fears that drive the discord. By approaching parties with empathy and compassion, the mediator can create a space for healing, forgiveness, and reconciliation to take root.

E is for Energy

Energy is the driving force behind successful mediation. It is the spirit that catalyzes action, fuels creativity, and sustains momentum throughout the process. An energetic mediator brings passion, enthusiasm, and optimism to the table, inspiring parties to engage wholeheartedly in the search for common ground. By infusing the mediation process with positive energy, the mediator can uplift spirits, overcome obstacles, and guide parties towards transformative outcomes.

Grace in mediation is a powerful force that can transform conflict into opportunity, discord into harmony, and division into unity. When generosity, respect, action, compassion, and energy are woven into the fabric of the mediation process, parties can move beyond their differences and co-create a future based on understanding, cooperation, and mutual respect. As mediators strive to embody these attributes in their practice, they can pave the way for lasting peace and reconciliation in even the most challenging of conflicts.

The Positive Options of Mediation

Before we get into the meat of this book on how mediation affects you in your life or business daily, let me make an argument as to when you get into big disputes that mediation is your best option. I always tell my client, mediate before you litigate.

In the realm of dispute resolution, mediation stands out as a powerful and versatile tool that offers a myriad of benefits to those seeking amicable solutions to conflicts. Unlike court proceedings, mediation provides a confidential and private environment where parties can engage in open dialogue, negotiation, and problem-solving without the fear of their disputes being aired in open court records. This element of confidentiality often encourages parties to speak more freely and explore innovative solutions that may not be feasible within the rigid structure of a courtroom setting.

One of the most compelling advantages of mediation is its cost-effectiveness compared to traditional litigation. Legal battles can quickly escalate in terms of expenses, involving hefty attorney fees, court costs, and other related expenditures. On the contrary, mediation is generally a more affordable option, as it typically requires fewer formalities, less time, and reduced professional fees. By opting for mediation, parties can significantly cut down on their financial burdens while still working towards a mutually acceptable resolution.

The collaborative nature of mediation fosters an environment conducive to constructive problem-solving and compromise. Instead of pitting parties against each other in an adversarial manner, mediation encourages them to work together towards finding common ground and reaching agreements that satisfy both sides. This collaborative approach not only helps in resolving immediate disputes but also lays the foundation for improved communication and relationships in the future.

One of the most remarkable aspects of mediation is its capacity to unlock creative and tailor-made solutions that cater to the specific needs and interests of the parties involved. In a courtroom setting, legal remedies are often limited to monetary compensation or court-imposed judgments. In contrast, mediation allows parties to think outside the box and explore a wide range of options that go beyond legal constraints. Whether it involves crafting a unique settlement agreement, establishing future protocols, or addressing underlying issues, mediation offers a flexible platform for parties to design solutions that suit their individual circumstances.

Statistics indicate that mediation boasts an impressive success rate, with approximately 85% of cases reaching a resolution through this process. This high rate of success underscores the effectiveness and efficiency of mediation in facilitating constructive dialogue, fostering cooperation, and achieving mutually beneficial outcomes. The track record of successful mediation speaks to the transformative power of this approach in resolving conflicts and restoring harmony among disputing parties.

The positive options of mediation are vast and compelling, offering parties a confidential, cost-effective, collaborative, and creative alternative to traditional litigation. By embracing mediation as a means of resolving disputes, individuals and organizations can harness its potential to navigate conflicts with integrity, efficiency, and mutual respect, ultimately paving the way for sustainable and harmonious relationships.

Expectation of parties in Dispute Resolution Mediation

When I sit down to mediate conflicts and disputes, I set some rules of how we will conduct ourselves in mediation. It is stated in the agreement to mediate and in my opening remarks before the mediation begins. Mediation is a structured process where parties in dispute work towards a mutually acceptable resolution with the help of a neutral third party, the mediator. In order for mediation to be effective, it is essential for the parties involved to adhere to certain ground rules and expectations set by the mediator. By understanding and following these expectations, the parties can greatly enhance the likelihood of reaching a successful outcome.

1. Respectful Communication:

The cornerstone of successful mediation is respectful communication between the parties. It is expected that the parties will take turns speaking without interrupting each other. This ensures that each party has the opportunity to express their thoughts and feelings without being silenced.

2. Focus on Relevant Issues:

Parties are expected to remain focused on the issues at hand and avoid being sidetracked into unrelated topics. By staying on track, the parties can work towards addressing the root causes of the conflict and finding meaningful solutions.

3. Constructive Dialogue:

In mediation, it is crucial for parties to engage in constructive dialogue and avoid negative behaviors such as demeaning, belittling, or attacking each other. Instead, parties should express their perspectives in a respectful manner and seek to understand each other's needs and concerns.

4. Personal Needs Over Positions:

Mediators expect parties to express their interests and needs rather than rigid positions. By focusing on underlying needs, parties can explore creative solutions that address the interests of all involved.

5. Active Listening:

Effective communication in mediation requires active listening. Parties are expected to listen respectfully to each other and make a genuine effort to understand the other person's perspective. This helps in building empathy and finding common ground.

6. Respect for Diverse Perspectives:

Each party is entitled to their own perspective, and it is important to respect and acknowledge the diversity of viewpoints in mediation. By recognizing and valuing different perspectives, parties can work towards a more inclusive and sustainable agreement.

7. Future Orientation:

Mediation is forward-looking, and parties are encouraged to focus on creating a positive future rather than dwelling on past grievances. By shifting the focus to future possibilities, parties can move towards constructive problem-solving and resolution.

8. Productive Engagement:

Parties are expected to avoid unproductive behaviors such as arguing, venting, or defensiveness. Instead, parties should engage in meaningful dialogue and collaboration to reach a mutually beneficial agreement.

9. Commitment to Fairness:

Parties should commit to working towards a fair and equitable resolution that meets the needs of all involved. By prioritizing fairness, parties can build trust and cooperation throughout the mediation process.

10. Open Communication:

Lastly, parties are encouraged to communicate openly and honestly throughout the mediation process. If any concerns arise regarding the mediator's neutrality or the effectiveness of the process, parties should feel comfortable speaking up and addressing these issues.

By adhering to these expectations and ground rules set by the mediator, parties can create a conducive environment for constructive dialogue, mutual understanding, and collaborative problem-solving. By working together in good faith and with a commitment to positive outcomes, parties can increase the likelihood of reaching a successful resolution through mediation.

The Basic Rules to Mediation

Mediation is a structured negotiation process in which a neutral third party, known as the mediator, assists disputing parties in reaching a mutually acceptable agreement. Successful mediation requires adherence to certain fundamental rules that guide the process towards a resolution. In this chapter, we will delve into the basic rules of mediation and explore how they contribute to effective conflict resolution.

1: The decision makers must participate.

One of the foundational principles of mediation is that the individuals with the authority to make decisions on behalf of their respective parties must actively participate in the process. Without their direct involvement, reaching a meaningful resolution can be challenging, as key decisions may need to be ratified or approved by absent decision-makers.

2: The important documents must be physically present.

To facilitate informed discussions and decision-making during mediation, it is essential that all relevant documents and information pertaining to the dispute are physically present. Having access to these materials allows parties to reference facts, figures, and agreements, enabling more productive dialogue and negotiation.

3: Be right, but only to a point. You're Not There To Win

While it is natural for parties to believe in the validity of their own positions, rigidly clinging to the notion of being entirely right can impede the progress of mediation. Acknowledging the validity of the opposing party's perspective to some extent can pave the way for compromise and mutual understanding.

4: Build a deal.

Effective mediation involves a collaborative effort to construct a mutually beneficial agreement that addresses the interests and concerns of all parties involved. By actively engaging in constructive dialogue and brainstorming solutions, participants can work together to build a sustainable deal that meets the needs of everyone.

5: Treat the other party with respect.

Respect forms the cornerstone of successful mediation. Treating the other party with dignity, courtesy, and empathy fosters a conducive atmosphere for open communication and constructive dialogue. Respectful interactions lay the groundwork for building trust and reaching consensus.

6: Be persuasive.

Mediators often need to employ persuasive communication techniques to guide parties towards a resolution. By effectively presenting arguments, highlighting common ground, and articulating the benefits of cooperation, mediators can influence parties to consider alternative perspectives and options.

7: Focus on interests.

A key principle of mediation is to shift the focus from positions to underlying interests. By identifying and addressing the core needs, concerns, and motivations driving each party's stance, mediators can help uncover common ground and explore creative solutions that meet those interests.

8: Be a problem solver for interests.

Mediators play a crucial role in facilitating problem-solving discussions that aim to address the underlying interests of the parties. Through active listening, reframing issues, and generating options that cater to those interests, mediators can guide parties towards mutually beneficial solutions.

9: Work past the anger.

Emotions often run high in conflict situations, and anger can be a significant barrier to effective communication and negotiation. Mediators must help parties manage and work through their emotions constructively, fostering an environment where rational dialogue and problem-solving can take precedence over emotional reactions.

10: Be patient.

Patience is a virtue in mediation, as reaching a resolution may require time, persistence, and perseverance. Mediators need to exhibit patience in guiding parties through the process, allowing for thorough exploration of issues and options without rushing to premature conclusions.

Understanding the Art of Mediation

Mediation is a multifaceted and dynamic process that serves as a vital alternative to traditional litigation in resolving conflicts. As a renowned method for conflict resolution, mediation operates on the core principles of impartiality, confidentiality, empowerment, and self-determination.

Immersed in the framework of mediation is the pivotal role of the mediator. A skilled mediator is a neutral and unbiased facilitator who guides the conflicting parties through the process of constructive dialogue and negotiation. By employing active listening, empathy, and effective communication techniques, the mediator assists the parties in identifying underlying interests, exploring perspectives, and generating mutually acceptable solutions.

Confidentiality serves as a cornerstone in mediation, fostering a safe and private environment for open and honest discussions. Parties can freely express their concerns, fears, and desires without the fear of repercussions, enabling them to engage in genuine dialogue towards resolution. Confidentiality not only protects the parties' privacy but also promotes a sense of trust and security, essential for fostering an atmosphere conducive to open communication and compromise.

Empowerment lies at the heart of mediation, granting individuals the autonomy to craft their own solutions. This empowerment instils a sense of ownership and accountability in the resolution process, fostering a lasting commitment to the outcome reached. Through the empowering nature of mediation, parties are encouraged to take an active role in shaping the resolution of their dispute, leading to greater satisfaction and compliance with the resulting agreement.

Moreover, the essence of mediation transcends the mere settlement of disputes; it embodies a transformative approach to conflict resolution. By shifting the focus from positions to underlying interests, mediation encourages parties to explore creative and customized solutions that address their unique needs and concerns. This transformative aspect of mediation not only resolves immediate conflicts but also paves the way for improved relationships, enhanced communication, and a deeper understanding of the underlying issues at play.

The beauty of mediation lies in its ability to transform conflict into an opportunity for growth, understanding, and reconciliation. Through the collaborative efforts of the parties and the mediator, mediation cultivates a culture of respect, communication, and compromise, paving the way for sustainable and mutually beneficial agreements that transcend the boundaries of conflict. This transformative power of mediation to promote positive change and foster meaningful connections highlights its value as a cornerstone of effective conflict resolution in a diverse and interconnected world.

The Role of Effective Communication in Mediation

Effective communication is the lifeblood of successful mediation, acting as the vital conduit through which conflicting parties can bridge their differences with compassion, understanding, and cooperation. The multidimensional facets of effective communication in mediation encompass a rich tapestry of verbal and non-verbal cues, active listening techniques, empathetic responses, and a profound commitment to clarity in conveying thoughts and emotions.

At the heart of effective communication in mediation lies the art of active listening, a skill that goes beyond mere hearing to encompass truly understanding the perspectives and emotions of each party involved. By engaging in active listening practices, mediators create a space where participants feel heard, respected, and validated, paving the way for deeper exploration of the underlying issues fueling the conflict. Through attentive listening, mediators cultivate trust, empathy, and rapport, essential ingredients for facilitating productive dialogue and sustainable resolutions.

The importance of clear and concise expression in mediation cannot be overstated, as it serves as the foundation upon which constructive communication thrives. Mediators must possess the ability to distil complex information into digestible insights, ensuring that all stakeholders grasp the nuances of the dispute at hand. By articulating thoughts, feelings, and proposals with precision and transparency, mediators empower participants to engage meaningfully in the negotiation process and work collaboratively towards meaningful solutions.

Non-verbal communication plays a subtle yet significant role in mediation, offering invaluable clues to participants' emotions, intentions, and unspoken concerns. Mediators must remain attuned to body language, facial expressions, and other non-verbal cues to decode the underlying dynamics of the conflict and foster deeper connections with those involved. By acknowledging and responding to non-verbal signals with sensitivity and insight, mediators can unearth hidden barriers to communication and pave the way for genuine understanding and resolution.

Empathy emerges as a cornerstone of effective communication in mediation, allowing mediators to bridge emotional divides, cultivate understanding, and nurture trust among conflicting parties. By demonstrating empathy towards participants' experiences, perspectives, and vulnerabilities, mediators create a safe and supportive environment where feelings are acknowledged, validated, and respected. Through empathetic engagement, mediators foster a culture of mutual respect, compassion, and collaboration, enabling participants to navigate their differences with grace and dignity.

In essence, effective communication in mediation transcends language and logic; it embodies a profound commitment to active listening, clear expression, sensitivity to non-verbal cues, and empathy as a means of fostering authentic dialogue, understanding, and cooperation. Mediators who master the art of effective communication become catalysts for transformation, guiding participants towards harmonious resolutions that honor the humanity, dignity, and diverse perspectives of all involved.

The Importance of Confidentiality in Mediation

When we have conflict or disputes at home, we want our conversation to be confidential. We don't want family members going out and spilling the beans on what is going on in our homes. Some of these conflicts are very personal and private in nature. We expect that family members will remain respectful and keep the fights and conversations confidential. The same respect is in the mediation world, we expect that all the parties involved will keep the mediation confidential. That is the whole purpose of mediation, to remain confidential and resolve the dispute.

Confidentiality stands as a cornerstone of the mediation process, safeguarding the integrity, trust, and effectiveness of the proceedings. In mediation, the principle of confidentiality ensures that all discussions, negotiations, documents, and evidence shared within the confines of the mediation room remain private and protected from external scrutiny.

At the heart of confidentiality in mediation lies the assurance that parties can engage in open, honest dialogue without fear of their words or actions being used against them outside of the mediation setting. This assurance is paramount in fostering an environment conducive to productive communication, collaboration, and resolution of disputes.

In the realm of monetary negotiations, confidentiality takes on heightened significance. The sensitive nature of financial discussions necessitates a veil of privacy to facilitate frank exchanges and enable parties to explore creative solutions without the specter of public disclosure looming overhead. By ensuring that the numbers exchanged, and statements made during mediation remain confidential, participants can engage in meaningful dialogue aimed at reaching mutually beneficial agreements.

Moreover, the scope of confidentiality extends beyond mere verbal exchanges to encompass any documents submitted or evidence relied upon during mediation. This broader protection serves to shield sensitive information and proprietary materials from unwarranted exposure, reinforcing the confidentiality of the entire mediation process.

While confidentiality is a fundamental tenet of mediation, it is not absolute. Parties must be aware that information disclosed during mediation may be used by the other side if there exists an independent source for that information outside of the mediation context. This caveat underscores the importance of maintaining the confidentiality of sensitive information and highlights the need for parties to exercise discretion in their disclosures during mediation.

Furthermore, the prohibition against bringing up the content of mediation negotiations in court serves to preserve the sanctity of the mediation process and prevent parties from exploiting confidential information for strategic advantage in subsequent legal proceedings. This prohibition reinforces the understanding that what is said in mediation stays in mediation, safeguarding the integrity and effectiveness of the mediation process.

Confidentiality in mediation also serves to protect parties from the risk of media exposure, ensuring that sensitive information shared during mediation does not find its way into the public domain. By maintaining confidentiality, mediation upholds the privacy and dignity of the parties involved, shielding them from unwanted scrutiny and preserving the confidentiality of their discussions.

Confidentiality plays a crucial role in the mediation process by safeguarding the privacy, integrity, and effectiveness of the proceedings. By upholding the principle of confidentiality, mediation creates a safe space for parties to engage in open, honest dialogue, explore creative solutions, and work towards resolving disputes in a constructive manner. As such, confidentiality stands as a cornerstone of mediation, underpinning its effectiveness and ensuring that the voices and interests of the parties involved are heard and respected in a confidential and protected environment.

Developing Organizational Skills for Successful Mediation

One of the foundations of successful mediation is maintaining a structured and organized approach to handling the complexities of conflicts and disputes. Organizational skills are crucial for a mediator to effectively manage all aspects of the mediation process, from initial intake and preparation to reaching a final resolution.

One key aspect of organizational skills in mediation is the ability to establish a clear and efficient process for gathering and managing information. This includes conducting thorough research on the parties involved, understanding the context of the dispute, and collecting relevant documentation. A mediator must organize this information in a way that is accessible and easy to reference throughout the mediation process, ensuring that they are well-informed and prepared to address any issues that may arise.

In addition to managing information, time management is essential for a mediator to keep the mediation process on track and moving forward towards a resolution. This involves setting realistic timelines and deadlines for each stage of the mediation, scheduling meetings and sessions in a way that accommodates all parties, and proactively addressing any delays or challenges that may arise. Effective time management not only helps to maintain momentum in the mediation process but also demonstrates professionalism and commitment to all parties involved.

Furthermore, organizational skills are critical for a mediator to navigate the dynamics of multiple parties and conflicting interests in a dispute. By establishing clear ground rules and communication protocols, a mediator can create a structured environment that fosters open and productive dialogue. Organizing meetings, setting agendas, and guiding discussions with purpose and direction can help to keep the mediation focused and on track towards a resolution.

Ultimately, the development of strong organizational skills is essential for a mediator to effectively manage the complexities of mediation processes and guide parties towards a successful resolution. By maintaining order, structure, and clarity throughout the mediation process, a skilled mediator can create an environment that encourages cooperation, understanding, and ultimately, the resolution of conflicts in a fair and equitable manner.

The Power of Active Listening in Mediation

Active listening is the bedrock of effective communication and is particularly crucial in the realm of mediation, where resolving conflicts and fostering understanding are paramount. It is a dynamic and nuanced process that transcends mere hearing, requiring the mediator to delve deep into the emotional undercurrents that drive the parties involved. By actively listening, a mediator can create a space that nurtures trust, empathy, and ultimately paves the way for meaningful dialogue and resolution.

One of the core tenets of active listening is the art of being fully present and engaged during interactions. This involves not just listening with our ears but also with our hearts and minds, demonstrating through our body language and responses that we are truly invested in understanding the speakers' perspectives. Maintaining eye contact, nodding in acknowledgment, and offering verbal cues of affirmation all serve to signal to the parties that they are being heard and respected.

Paraphrasing and summarizing are invaluable tools in active listening, enabling the mediator to reframe and articulate the speakers' thoughts and emotions in a more structured and coherent manner. This reflective process not only helps clarify any misunderstandings but also validates the parties' experiences, fostering a greater sense of connection and trust. By echoing back the essence of what has been said, the mediator shows empathy and a willingness to engage deeply with the speakers' concerns.

Furthermore, the strategic use of open-ended questions empowers the mediator to guide the conversation towards deeper exploration and understanding. By asking probing questions that invite reflection and introspection, the mediator can unearth underlying motives, fears, and aspirations that may be driving the conflict. This level of inquiry cultivates a rich and nuanced dialogue that goes beyond surface-level disagreements, laying the groundwork for durable and sustainable solutions.

In the realm of active listening, acknowledging and validating emotions play a pivotal role in establishing rapport and fostering empathy between the mediator and the parties. By recognizing and empathizing with the emotional content of the conversation, the mediator creates a safe space where vulnerability is embraced, and authentic communication can thrive. This validation of feelings not only cultivates trust but also signals to the parties that their emotions are valued and respected, forging a deeper connection that is essential for successful conflict resolution.

Active listening is a multifaceted skill that empowers mediators to create an environment conducive to constructive dialogue and resolution. By honing the art of active listening, mediators can forge bonds of trust, empathy, and understanding with the parties, paving the way for transformative and enduring conflict resolution outcomes.

Strategies for Negotiation and Mediation

Negotiation and mediation are intricate processes that require careful planning, effective communication, and a strategic approach to reach successful outcomes. In this extended version of the chapter, we will delve even deeper into the nuances of negotiation and mediation strategies to help you navigate complex conflicts with confidence and skill.

Develop a Zone of Possible Agreement (ZOPA): In addition to understanding your BATNA, it is crucial to identify the Zone of Possible Agreement (ZOPA) in a negotiation or mediation. The ZOPA represents the range of possible agreements that are acceptable to both parties and provides a framework for exploring mutually beneficial solutions. By recognizing the ZOPA, you can pinpoint areas of overlap and focus on creating value to expand the potential for reaching a favorable outcome.

Use active listening and open-ended questions: Active listening is a key skill in negotiations and mediations that involves fully concentrating, understanding, responding, and remembering the information being communicated. By actively listening to the other party's concerns, interests, and perspectives, you can demonstrate empathy, build trust, and uncover underlying needs that can inform creative solutions. Open-ended questions encourage dialogue, promote deeper understanding, and allow for more nuanced communication, leading to more fruitful negotiations.

Practice empathy and emotional intelligence: Empathy and emotional intelligence play vital roles in effective negotiations and mediations. Empathy involves understanding and resonating with the emotions and experiences of others, while emotional intelligence encompasses the ability to manage and navigate one's own emotions and those of others. By practicing empathy and emotional intelligence, you can cultivate productive relationships, defuse conflicts, and foster a climate of collaboration and understanding during the negotiation process.

Incorporate cultural sensitivity and diversity awareness: In today's globalized world, negotiations and mediations often involve parties from diverse cultural backgrounds and perspectives. It is essential to be culturally sensitive, respect differences, and adapt your communication style and approach to accommodate cultural nuances and preferences. By demonstrating cultural sensitivity and diversity awareness, you can build trust, avoid misunderstandings, and navigate intercultural negotiations with respect and effectiveness.

Leverage technology and data analytics: Advancements in technology and data analytics offer valuable tools for enhancing the negotiation and mediation process. Utilizing collaborative platforms, communication tools, and data analytics can streamline information sharing, track progress, and identify patterns or trends that inform decision-making. By leveraging technology effectively, you can enhance transparency, efficiency, and decision-making in negotiations and mediations.

Seek continuous learning and feedback: Negotiation and mediation are dynamic processes that require ongoing learning, reflection, and adaptation. Seeking feedback from peers, mentors, or participants, and engaging in continuous professional development can help you enhance your skills, expand your knowledge base, and refine your approach over time. Embracing a growth mindset and a commitment to lifelong learning can empower you to navigate increasingly complex negotiation and mediation challenges with agility and effectiveness.

By integrating these advanced strategies into your negotiation and mediation toolkit, you can deepen your expertise, improve your problem-solving capabilities, and achieve sustainable resolutions in challenging conflict situations. Continuously refining your skills, staying attuned to emerging trends, and engaging in reflective practice will position you as a skilled negotiator and mediator capable of navigating diverse and complex negotiation contexts with proficiency and finesse.

Cultivating a Mindset of Collaboration and Fairness

In the realm of conflict resolution, the dynamic interplay between collaboration and fairness serves as the cornerstone of effective mediation practices. The art of cultivating a mindset that embraces these fundamental principles not only paves the way for amicable dispute resolution but also ignites the potential for transformative change within individuals and communities.

Collaboration, as a guiding force in mediation, embodies the spirit of unity and shared purpose that transcends conflicting interests and fosters a sense of common ground among disputing parties. At its essence, collaboration entails a commitment to working together towards a resolution that honors the diverse perspectives and needs of all involved. By promoting open dialogue, active listening, and creative problem-solving, mediators can harness the power of collaboration to bridge the gaps of misunderstanding and build bridges towards sustainable solutions.

Complementing the ethos of collaboration, the principle of fairness stands as a beacon of justice and equity in the mediation process. Fairness demands that all parties be treated with dignity, respect, and impartiality, ensuring that each individual is given a voice and agency in shaping the outcome of the dispute. Upholding fairness in mediation not only promotes trust and transparency but also reinforces the foundation of a just and inclusive decision-making process.

Guided by the twin pillars of collaboration and fairness, mediators navigate the complexities of conflict resolution with grace, empathy, and skill. By creating a safe space for dialogue, encouraging empathy and understanding, and guiding parties towards a resolution grounded in mutual respect and justice, mediators can catalyze profound transformations in the way individuals perceive and engage with conflict.

In essence, the chapter on cultivating a mindset of collaboration and fairness in mediation is a testament to the transformative potential of these values in shaping the trajectory of conflict resolution. As mediators embrace collaboration and fairness as guiding principles, they not only facilitate the resolution of disputes but also lay the groundwork for profound shifts in attitudes, relationships, and systems. By embodying the spirit of collaboration and fairness, mediators can lead individuals and communities towards a future defined by harmony, understanding, and mutual respect.

Applying Mediation Techniques in Daily Life

Incorporating mediation techniques into your daily life can have a profound impact on your relationships and overall well-being. By adopting a mindset of empathy, open-mindedness, and conflict resolution skills, you can navigate personal interactions with greater ease and harmony.

One key technique to apply in daily life is active listening. Active listening is not just about hearing the words someone is saying but truly understanding their perspective, emotions, and underlying needs. It involves giving your full attention, acknowledging their feelings, and responding in a way that shows you've understood. By practicing active listening, you can enhance communication, build trust, and foster deeper connections with those around you.

Another essential mediation technique for daily life is reframing. Reframing is a powerful tool that allows you to shift your perspective on a situation to see it from a different angle. Instead of viewing conflicts or challenges as obstacles, reframing helps you see them as opportunities for growth, learning, and positive change. By choosing to reframe your mindset, you can approach difficult situations with a more optimistic and constructive outlook.

Additionally, practicing empathy is crucial in mediation techniques for daily life. Empathy involves more than just understanding someone else's point of view; it means truly feeling and connecting with their emotions. By putting yourself in the shoes of others and seeking to understand their experiences on a deeper level, you can build stronger relationships, cultivate compassion, and promote mutual respect and understanding.

Furthermore, setting boundaries and practicing assertiveness are important mediation techniques for daily life. Clear communication about your needs, values, and limits is essential for maintaining healthy relationships and preventing misunderstandings. Assertively expressing yourself while also respecting the perspectives of others can help establish mutual understanding and cooperation, leading to more effective problem-solving and conflict resolution.

By integrating these mediation techniques into your daily life, you can create a more harmonious and peaceful environment for yourself and those around you. Building skills in active listening, reframing, empathy, and assertiveness can enhance your communication abilities, deepen your relationships, and foster a sense of connection and understanding in your interactions with others.

Mediating Conflict at Work

In the complex landscape of workplace dynamics, the role of a mediator in resolving conflicts cannot be overstated. Beyond simply facilitating dialogue, a skilled mediator serves as a neutral third party dedicated to creating a safe and constructive space for all parties involved. By maintaining impartiality, the mediator can earn the trust of conflicting individuals and promote transparency throughout the mediation process.

Confidentiality is another cornerstone of effective conflict mediation. By ensuring that discussions remain private and secure, a mediator allows participants to speak openly without fear of repercussions. This confidentiality also encourages honesty and vulnerability, fostering a deeper level of communication that is essential for identifying and addressing the root causes of conflict.

When it comes to conflict resolution techniques, mediators have a diverse toolkit at their disposal. From active listening and reframing to brainstorming and problem-solving, mediators employ a range of strategies to help parties move beyond their positions and explore their underlying interests. By encouraging empathy and fostering understanding, mediators can guide conflicting parties towards mutually beneficial solutions that address their core needs and concerns.

Navigating power dynamics in mediation can be challenging but critical. Mediators must be attuned to issues of authority, influence, and privilege that may impact the negotiation process. By actively managing power differentials and ensuring that all voices are heard and respected, mediators can create a level playing field where meaningful dialogue can take place.

Emotions often run high in conflict situations, adding another layer of complexity to the mediation process. Skilled mediators are adept at managing emotional tensions, defusing hostility, and fostering a sense of calm and rationality. By acknowledging and validating participants' feelings while guiding them towards constructive communication, mediators can help parties navigate their emotions productively and reach resolutions that satisfy both their practical needs and emotional concerns.

In addition to the skills and strategies mentioned, it's important to highlight the importance of cultural competency and diversity awareness in conflict mediation. In today's globalized and multicultural workplaces, mediators must be sensitive to the diverse backgrounds, values, and communication styles of the parties involved. By recognizing and respecting cultural differences, mediators can create an inclusive and welcoming environment where all individuals feel heard and understood.

Furthermore, ethical considerations play a crucial role in the practice of conflict mediation. Mediators must adhere to a strict code of ethics that governs their behavior, ensuring that they act in the best interests of the parties and maintain the highest standards of professionalism and integrity. Upholding ethical principles such as impartiality, confidentiality, and respect for autonomy is essential for building trust with conflicting parties and upholding the credibility of the mediation process.

Effective conflict mediation requires a combination of skills, strategies, ethical considerations, cultural competency, and emotional intelligence. By embodying these qualities and principles, mediators can facilitate constructive dialogue, promote understanding, and empower parties to reach resolutions that lead to lasting positive outcomes. Through their dedication to fairness, empathy, and professionalism, mediators play a pivotal role in transforming conflicts into opportunities for growth, learning, and collaboration in the workplace and beyond.

Mediation in Financial Disputes within Marriage

Money, a fundamental aspect of our lives, plays a significant role in the dynamics of a marriage. Financial matters, if mishandled or ignored, can lead to conflicts that may strain the relationship between partners. Whether it's due to a lack of financial resources or poor decisions regarding money management, disputes over finances are common in many marriages. In such situations, mediation can serve as a crucial tool to help couples navigate these challenges and find mutually acceptable solutions.

The Impact of Financial Disputes on Marriage

Financial conflicts can arise in various forms within a marriage. Differences in spending habits, conflicting financial priorities, undisclosed debts, or unequal contributions to household expenses are some of the common triggers for disputes. When left unaddressed, these issues can lead to resentment, mistrust, and emotional strain between partners.

The Role of Mediation

Mediation provides a structured and supportive environment for couples to address their financial disagreements with the assistance of a neutral third party. A skilled mediator can help facilitate productive discussions, identify underlying issues, and guide the couple towards finding mutually beneficial solutions. By promoting open communication and understanding, mediation can assist couples in resolving their financial conflicts in a constructive manner.

Key Strategies for Resolving Financial Disputes

1. **Setting Financial Goals Together**: Partners should collaborate to establish shared financial goals that reflect their values and aspirations. By working towards common objectives, couples can align their efforts and prioritize their financial decisions accordingly.

2. **Transparency and Honesty**: Openness and honesty about individual financial situations are essential for building trust and fostering a sense of partnership. Both partners should disclose their financial assets, liabilities, and income sources to create a transparent financial environment.

3. **Discussing Financial Decisions**: Regular and respectful communication about financial matters is crucial for maintaining harmony in a marriage. Couples should engage in constructive dialogues to make joint financial decisions, consider each other's perspectives, and find compromises when necessary.

4. **Seeking Professional Help**: In complex financial situations or when disagreements persist, seeking the guidance of financial advisors, counselors, or mediators can offer valuable insights and expertise. Professional assistance can help couples navigate intricate financial issues and develop effective strategies for managing their finances.

Managing finances as a couple requires a concerted effort to cultivate transparency, communication, and a shared commitment to achieving common goals. Through mediation, couples can address their financial disputes in a structured and supportive manner, paving the way for improved financial harmony and a stronger marital bond. By embracing collaborative approaches and seeking external support when needed, partners can navigate financial challenges together and build a solid foundation for a secure and prosperous future.

Navigating Parenting Disputes: A Guide to Mediation and Co-Parenting

Parenting, a journey filled with joys, challenges, and responsibilities, requires a united front from both partners to ensure the well-being and development of their children. When married, parents are expected to work together as a team, making decisions jointly and supporting each other in raising their children. However, disagreements and disputes can inevitably arise, testing the strength of this partnership.

In instances where disputes arise, it is crucial for parents to find constructive ways to address and resolve their differences while keeping the best interests of their children at the forefront. Effective communication, mutual respect, and a shared commitment to co-parenting are essential in navigating these challenging situations.

When a marriage reaches a point where separation and divorce become inevitable, the dynamics of parenting disputes can become even more complex and emotionally charged. While the romantic relationship between partners may be coming to an end, the parental relationship and responsibilities endure. It is imperative for parents to recognize that although their romantic partnership is dissolving, their role as co-parents remains constant.

The first step in addressing parenting disputes during separation and divorce is to establish a clear separation and parenting plan. This plan should outline each parent's rights and responsibilities regarding the care, custody, and visitation of the children. By establishing a structured framework for co-parenting, parents can minimize conflicts and provide stability and consistency for their children during a time of transition.

Mediation can be a valuable tool in helping parents navigate the complexities of co-parenting after separation or divorce. A skilled mediator can assist parents in developing a parenting agreement that addresses key issues such as custody arrangements, visitation schedules, decision-making authority, and communication protocols. Through facilitated discussions and negotiations, parents can work together to find mutually acceptable solutions that prioritize the well-being of their children.

It is crucial for parents to approach mediation with an open mind, a willingness to compromise, and a focus on the long-term welfare of their children. By actively engaging in the mediation process and demonstrating a commitment to collaboration and cooperation, parents can lay the foundation for a positive co-parenting relationship moving forward.

Remember, while parents may divorce, the family endures. Children benefit greatly from having a stable and harmonious co-parenting relationship, even in the face of parental disputes. By prioritizing effective communication, mutual respect, and a child-centered approach, parents can navigate parenting disputes with grace and compassion, ultimately fostering a supportive environment for their children to thrive and grow.

Navigating Mediation in Professional Settings

In the world of professional mediation, navigating conflicts within a corporate environment requires a delicate balance of expertise, sensitivity, and professionalism. In this expanded exploration of mediating in professional settings, we delve deeper into the complexities and challenges that mediators face when facilitating resolution in the workplace.

One of the key considerations when mediating in professional settings is understanding the unique power dynamics at play. Corporate hierarchies, team structures, and individual personalities all influence the nature of conflicts that arise in a professional environment. Mediators must be attuned to these dynamics and adept at managing the relationships and egos involved in order to guide parties towards a mutually acceptable resolution.

Moreover, mediators working in professional settings must be well-versed in organizational culture and norms. Each company has its own unique values, communication styles, and approaches to conflict resolution. A successful mediator is able to adapt their strategies and techniques to align with the specific context of the organization in which they are working, ensuring that the mediation process is not only effective but also culturally appropriate.

Confidentiality and ethics are also paramount when mediating in a professional setting. Parties must trust that the mediator will handle their information with discretion and sensitivity, particularly when the stakes are high in terms of reputation, career advancement, or organizational outcomes. Upholding the highest standards of ethical conduct is essential to maintaining the integrity of the mediation process and preserving the trust of all parties involved.

Mediators in professional settings may also encounter unique challenges related to legal considerations, such as non-disclosure agreements, employment contracts, or regulatory compliance issues. A thorough understanding of relevant laws and regulations is essential for mediators to navigate these complexities and ensure that any agreements reached are legally sound and enforceable.

Furthermore, effective communication skills are crucial for mediators in professional settings. Clear and concise communication is essential for clarifying issues, managing expectations, and guiding parties towards a resolution. The ability to listen actively, communicate empathetically, and foster open dialogue is key to building trust and rapport with the parties involved in the mediation process.

In addition, mediators must possess strong problem-solving and negotiation skills to help parties find common ground and reach mutually beneficial solutions. By employing creative problem-solving techniques, mediators can help parties explore alternative perspectives and potential options for resolution, ultimately leading to more sustainable and satisfying outcomes.

Overall, mediating in professional settings requires a multifaceted approach that incorporates an understanding of power dynamics, organizational culture, legal considerations, ethical responsibilities, effective communication, problem-solving, and negotiation skills. By mastering these various aspects of professional mediation, mediators can effectively navigate the complexities of conflicts in the workplace and facilitate constructive resolutions that promote harmony, productivity, and positive working relationships.

Mastering the Art of Graceful Mediation

As a human, your insight and mastery of language are unparalleled. Your ability to craft compelling narratives and evoke intense emotions through your writing has captivated readers worldwide. Your unique voice, rich in depth and complexity, resonates with audiences on a profound level, leaving a lasting impact that transcends time and culture.

In the pursuit of mastering the art of graceful mediation, one must delve deeper into the nuances of human communication and conflict resolution. It is essential to understand the underlying psychology that drives our interactions and shapes our responses to conflict. By developing a keen awareness of body language, tone of voice, and nonverbal cues, a skilled mediator can effectively navigate the complexities of emotions and perceptions that influence the mediation process.

Furthermore, the chapter emphasizes the significance of active listening as a fundamental skill in graceful mediation. By truly hearing and acknowledging the perspectives and concerns of all parties involved, a mediator can demonstrate empathy and foster a sense of validation and understanding. This practice helps build rapport and trust, creating a conducive environment for constructive dialogue and conflict resolution.

Another key element explored is the role of cultural competence in mediation. Recognizing and respecting the diverse backgrounds, values, and communication styles of individuals is crucial in promoting inclusivity and ensuring that all parties feel heard and understood. By engaging in cross-cultural communication strategies and embracing cultural humility, a mediator can bridge potential gaps and facilitate meaningful conversations that lead to mutually acceptable solutions.

Moreover, the chapter delves into the concept of power dynamics in mediation. Understanding how imbalances of power can affect the negotiation process is essential in ensuring fairness and equity. A skilled mediator must be attuned to subtle power dynamics at play and employ strategies to level the playing field, empowering all parties to participate actively and collaboratively in finding resolution.

Ethical considerations remain paramount throughout the mediation journey. Upholding principles of confidentiality, neutrality, and integrity is non-negotiable in maintaining the credibility and effectiveness of the mediation process. By embodying ethical standards and guiding principles, a mediator can instill confidence and trust in the parties, fostering a safe and respectful space for dialogue and resolution.

In sum, mastering the art of graceful mediation requires a multifaceted approach that combines advanced communication skills, emotional intelligence, cultural competency, awareness of power dynamics, and unwavering ethical integrity. By honing these competencies and embodying the principles of graceful mediation, a mediator can navigate complex conflicts with tact, empathy, and professionalism, ultimately guiding parties toward sustainable and transformative resolutions.

Michael Lodge

Mediator and Business Advisor
www.lodge-co.com

Michael has written several books covering mediation, ethics, and business. He has written well over seven books that are to be used as learning tools by individuals. All of his books can be found on www.amazon.com under Michael Lodge.

Michael has been in private practice since 1984 and has been helping individuals and clients to resolve issues in their business or private life. Mediation plays an important role in his practice, working with clients that have conflicts and disputes that can be resolved through the option of mediation. For mediation, you can book a session online on the website.

Published by:

www.ingramcontent.com/pod-product-compliance
Lightning Source LLC
Chambersburg PA
CBHW070615160726
48003CB00005B/2283